It Shall Pass

Coming Back to Life
after Losing Someone

WestBow Press books may be ordered through booksellers or by contacting:

WestBow Press
A Division of Thomas Nelson & Zondervan
1663 Liberty Drive
Bloomington, IN 47403
www.westbowpress.com
844-714-3454

Because of the dynamic nature of the Internet, any web addresses or links contained in this book may have changed since publication and may no longer be valid. The views expressed in this work are solely those of the author and do not necessarily reflect the views of the publisher, and the publisher hereby disclaims any responsibility for them.

Any people depicted in stock imagery provided by Getty Images are models, and such images are being used for illustrative purposes only.
Certain stock imagery © Getty Images.

Scripture quotations taken from The Holy Bible, New International Version® NIV® Copyright © 1973 1978 1984 2011 by Biblica, Inc. TM. Used by permission. All rights reserved worldwide.

ISBN: 979-8-3850-3078-1 (sc)
ISBN: 979-8-3850-3079-8 (hc)
ISBN: 979-8-3850-3080-4 (e)

Library of Congress Control Number: 2024916101

Print information available on the last page.

WestBow Press rev. date: 11/15/2024

WESTBOW
PRESS®
A DIVISION OF THOMAS NELSON
& ZONDERVAN

IN LOVING MEMORY OF

_____

In the loving memory of my late husband, Roberto Puig.
Forever and ever, to infinity and beyond!

Hello, I'm Sarah Martinez.

My decision to create this planner came after the unexpected passing of my husband, a healthy thirty-two-year-old man, who suddenly felt sick and passed away on a trip back home from Houston to Dallas, Texas, after a Thanksgiving weekend at his parents' house.

At this point in life, we were planning to get pregnant, we were preapproved to buy our first house, he was two weeks away from graduating from the chaplaincy course, and we were full of dreams and plans.

The night he passed felt like a strong slap on my face, throwing me miles away from everything I knew, from everything safe, and from everything that seemed to be God's plans. But since nothing is outside of God's plans, I've been learning to trust that my experiences can lead me to a deeper relationship with the Lord.

Even though I walk through the darkest valley, I will fear no evil, for you are with me; your rod and your staff, they comfort me.
—Psalm 23:4

If you have this planner in your hands, you are probably facing one of the hardest moments in your life. You may also be dealing with grief and trying to understand what just happened to your life. Maybe God answered no to you, and your entire world seems to be falling apart.

Whatever the situation is, it shall pass!

But during this journey, you will need to be constantly reminded that even when you don't understand God's plans, you are not alone, and you can trust that He knows the plan He has for you. It is a plan to prosper and not harm, a plan to give you hope and a future (Jeremiah 29:11).

The following pages are meant to help you get up and start moving forward. They will constantly remind you of God's promises, and you will have enough space to work on submitting your new plans, new dreams, and uncertain future to the solid rock, Jesus Christ.

May the Holy Spirit minister in your life through this planner.

Life is just a journey home!

LORD MEET ME IN MY
Secret Place

Take some time to write a letter to your loved one. Use this space to express all your emotions and start organizing your thoughts.

LORD MEET ME IN MY
Secret Place

Since ancient times no one has heard, no ear has perceived,
no eye has seen any God besides you, who acts
on behalf of those who wait for him.
—Isaiah 64:4

MY DAILY

Walk with God

And surely I am with you always,
to the very end of the age.
—Matthew 28:20

(S) (M) (T) (W) (T) (F) (S)   **DATE:** _____

Any urgent legal calls to make?

○

○

○

○

○

○

○

Self-Care Routine

❑ Take a shower.

❑ Eat breakfast, lunch, and
dinner.

Notes

God's presence with me didn't
change my reality. But in God,
I found my only resource,
hope, comfort, and peace.

GOD

Is healing you!

From time to time, you will feel a dense, heavy wave of
sadness and think you will live with this suffocating feeling for
the rest of your life. In these moments, trust in the Lord for,
"He cares for you" (1 Peter 5:7). Do not let
your feelings control your day.

Take some time to be honest about your
emotions, and present them all to the Lord.

Blessed are those who mourn, for they will be comforted.
—Matthew 5:4

He heals the brokenhearted and binds up their wounds.
—Psalm 147:3

GOD

Heal my pain

Do not be anxious about anything, but in every situation, by prayer and petition, with thanksgiving, present your requests to God. And the peace of God, which transcends all understanding, will guard your hearts and your minds in Christ Jesus.
—Philippians 4:6–7

MY DAILY
Walk with God

But blessed is the one who trusts in the Lord, whose confidence is in him.
—Jeremiah 17:7

(S) (M) (T) (W) (T) (F) (S)

DATE: _____

Books to Read:

○

○

○

○

○

○

○

○

○

○

○

Notes

- - - - - - - - - - - - - - - - - - -

- - - - - - - - - - - - - - - - - - -

- - - - - - - - - - - - - - - - - - -

- - - - - - - - - - - - - - - - - - -

Book suggestions:

Divine Disruption by Tony Evans
The Scars That Have Shaped Me by Vaneetha Risner

Take time to cry and allow yourself to express your emotions.

GOD
Heal my pain

GOD

Heal my pain

Save these pages to write a letter to yourself. Write here on the day you wake up full of hope, when your heart is full of joy (this day will come). Do it as a reminder of God's favor and grace and come back here when you need encouragement to keep moving. Use your testimony as proof that God is moving and working in your life.

Since ancient times no one has heard, no ear has perceived, no eye has seen any God besides you, who acts on behalf of those who wait for him.
—Isaiah 64:4

GOD

Heal my pain

He will wipe every tear from their eyes. There will be no more death or
mourning or crying or pain, for the old order of things has passed away.
—Revelation 21:4

GOD

Heal my pain

So do not fear, for I am with you; do not be dismayed, for I am your God.
I will strengthen you and help you; I will uphold you with my righteous right hand.
—Isaiah 41:10

MY DAILY

Walk with God

Commit to the Lord whatever you do,
and he will establish your plans.
—Proverbs 16:3

(S) (M) (T) (W) (T) (F) (S)   **DATE:** _____

New Plans and Dreams

- ◯
- ◯
- ◯
- ◯
- ◯
- ◯
- ◯

Self-Care Routine

- ❑ Change your clothes.
- ❑ Wash your face.
- ❑ Nourish your body.

Notes

- - - - - - - - - - - - - - - - -

- - - - - - - - - - - - - - - - -

- - - - - - - - - - - - - - - - -

- - - - - - - - - - - - - - - - -

Passwords to Remember

Allow yourself to feel the pain, knowing that healing is a journey, not a destination.

GOD
Is healing you!

It might take an extra step for you to start making plans and having new dreams. It may even feel inappropriate to have new plans that do not involve your loved one. But the more you plan, the more you can build your life back. It is the small steps you take that will take you far. Share your plans here.

He heals the brokenhearted and binds up their wounds.
—Psalm 147:3

GOD
Heal my pain

Cast all your anxiety on him because he cares for you.
—1 Peter 5:7

HE MAKES
everything new

MY DAILY
Walk with God

Have mercy on me, my God, have mercy on me, for in you I take refuge. I will take refuge in the shadow of your Wings until the disaster has passed.
—Psalm 57:1

(S) (M) (T) (W) (T) (F) (S)   **DATE:** _____

Subscriptions to Cancel:

○
○
○
○
○
○
○

Self-Care Routine

❏ Read a book.

❏ Take time to pray and find peace in the Lord.

Notes

- - - - - - - - - - - - - - - - - -

- - - - - - - - - - - - - - - - - -

- - - - - - - - - - - - - - - - - -

- - - - - - - - - - - - - - - - - -

Any subscriptions you can't cancel yet?

In the midst of my worst tribulation, I have found the very presence of the Lord as I never did before.

GOD

Heal my pain

Who of you by worrying can add a single hour to your life? Since you
cannot do this very little thing, why do you worry about the rest?
—Luke 12:25–26

HE MAKES
everything new

MY DAILY

Walk with God

Peace I leave with you; my peace I give
you. I do not give to you as the world gives.
Do not let your hearts be troubled and do
not be afraid.
——John 14:27

(S) (M) (T) (W) (T) (F) (S)   **DATE:** _____

Friends I Can Call:

○
○
○
○
○
○
○

Self-Care Routine

☐ Listen to a podcast.

☐ Stretch your body.

Notes

- -

- -

- -

- -

Prayer Request

**Take each day at a time,
allowing yourself the grace
to grieve and heal.**

GOD

Is healing you!

In some moments, you may question the purpose of your life and
your faith, and you may experience a huge void. It may seem
that despite your trust in the Lord, you still need to deal with
an immeasurable amount of pain, and it doesn't feel fair.

What I can share with you—and I keep reminding myself—is that it
may not be fair. Life is not fair, but it should not be a complete surprise
either. John 16:33 says, "In the world you will have tribulations, but
be of good cheer, I have overcome the world" (emphasis added).

God assured us that we would go through the desert, but He also
promised that we would not face this alone: "I am with you always,
even to the end of the age" (Matthew 28:20). God is with you right
now, amid the suffering, in the pain, and you will never be alone.

The Lord is close to the brokenhearted and saves those who are crushed in spirit.
—Psalm 34:18

GOD

Heal my pain

Have I not commanded you? Be strong and courageous. Do not be afraid; do not be discouraged, for the Lord your God will be with you wherever you go.
—Joshua 1:9

HE MAKES
everything new

MY DAILY

Walk with God

But he said to me, "My grace is sufficient for you, for my power is made perfect in weakness.
—2 Corinthians 12:9

(S) (M) (T) (W) (T) (F) (S)   **DATE:** _____

Moments to Remember

- ◯
- ◯
- ◯
- ◯
- ◯
- ◯
- ◯

Self-Care Routine

- ❑ Make your bed.
- ❑ Wash your hair.
- ❑ Light a candle.

Notes

- -
- -
- -
- -
- -
- -
- -

Embrace the grieving process knowing that it's OK to mourn and seek support.

GOD

Heal my pain

To be honest with you, sometimes I cannot see the future ahead of me. I'm scared, I'm afraid, and I'm experiencing a lack of control in my life. In these moments, all I can do is find in the Bible the answers for my soul. Where do you find hope for your difficult days?

Lord my God, I called to you for help, and you healed me.
—Psalm 30:2

MY DAILY
Walk with God

You, Lord, brought me up from the realm of the dead; you spared me From going down to the pit.
——Psalm 30:3

Ⓢ Ⓜ Ⓣ Ⓦ Ⓣ Ⓕ Ⓢ   **DATE:** _____

Places That Bring Good Memories

○
○
○
○
○
○
○

Write down a reminder for yourself.

‐‐‐‐‐‐‐‐‐‐‐‐‐‐‐‐‐‐‐‐‐‐‐‐‐‐‐‐‐

‐‐‐‐‐‐‐‐‐‐‐‐‐‐‐‐‐‐‐‐‐‐‐‐‐‐‐‐‐

‐‐‐‐‐‐‐‐‐‐‐‐‐‐‐‐‐‐‐‐‐‐‐‐‐‐‐‐‐

‐‐‐‐‐‐‐‐‐‐‐‐‐‐‐‐‐‐‐‐‐‐‐‐‐‐‐‐‐

‐‐‐‐‐‐‐‐‐‐‐‐‐‐‐‐‐‐‐‐‐‐‐‐‐‐‐‐‐

‐‐‐‐‐‐‐‐‐‐‐‐‐‐‐‐‐‐‐‐‐‐‐‐‐‐‐‐‐

Self-Care Routine

❑ Brew your morning coffee slowly.
❑ Make yourself a fruit platter.
❑ Go on a walk, even if it's just around the block.

> I sought the Lord and he answered me; he delivered me from all my fears.
> —Psalm 34:4

GOD

Heal my pain

Being strengthened with all power according to his glorious might
so that you may have great endurance and patience.
—Colossians 1:11

GOD

Heal my pain

Even if you don't believe or cannot see it yet, God is still on His throne. So, do not be rebellious to God's will. If God allowed you to go through this desert, He will also sustain you in this moment. Your pain will still be there, and that's fine, but do not let your pain have power over your life.

So with you: Now is your time of grief, but I will see you again
and you will rejoice, and no one will take away your joy.
—John 16:22

GOD
Heal my pain

You turned my wailing into dancing; you removed my sackcloth and clothed
me with joy, that my heart may sing your praises and not be silent.
Lord my God, I will praise you forever.
—Psalm 30:11–12

MY DAILY

Walk with God

Turn your ear to me, come quickly to
my rescue, be my rock of refuge, a strong
fortress to save me.
—Psalm 31:2

(S) (M) (T) (W) (T) (F) (S)   **DATE:** _____

Things You Are Not Ready to Do Yet

○

○

○

○

○

○

○

Self-Care Routine

❑ Find a quiet space to pray.

❑ Enroll in therapy.

❑ Make a playlist of your favorite
songs

Notes

Song Suggestion

(suggestions: "Quiet," Hillside Recording;
"Ruler," Hillside Recording).

**Embrace the tears, for
they carry the weight of
healing and release.**

GOD

Is healing me!

Don't be rebellious to God's will. Rebellion involves resisting authority and control. When you resist surrendering to Christ or accepting that God has different plans for your life, and you keep battling with God about why He allowed this tragedy to come into your life, it demonstrates that you have not yet surrendered to the Lord.

It is as if you were saying, "God, this time you chose the wrong person; you made a mistake." And we know that our God is sovereign and perfect in all His ways.

If He allowed you to go through this desert, He will also sustain you in this season. Is this the time when you need to take, to surrender all your plans to the Lord? Let Him reign over you!

I can do all this through him who gives me strength.
—Philippians 4:13

GOD
Heal my pain

I waited patiently for the Lord;
he turned to me and heard my cry.
—Psalm 40:1

GOD
Heal my pain

Be merciful to me, Lord, for I am in distress;
my eyes grow weak with sorrow, my soul and body with grief.
—Psalm 31:9

MY DAILY
Walk with God

But I trust in you, Lord
I say, "You are my God."
—Psalm 31:14

Ⓢ Ⓜ Ⓣ Ⓦ Ⓣ Ⓕ Ⓢ   **DATE:** _____

Reasons to Be Kind to Yourself

○

○

○

○

○

○

○

Self-Care Routine

❑ Engage in some self-directed therapy.

❑ Journal honestly.

❑ Text a trusted friend how you're feeling.

Notes

- -

- -

- -

- -

- -

- -

- -

**Celebrate your memories
and allow yourself space
for emotions that follow.**

Since ancient times no one has heard, no ear has perceived,
no eye has seen any God besides you, who acts on behalf of those who wait for him.
—Isaiah 64:4

GOD
Is healing me!

In the days you struggle to trust in God, and the upcoming days of your life seem to be drowning you, you may need to be reminded that at this point in your life, all you need and can do is wait for the Lord: "For since the beginning of the world, men have not heard nor perceived by the ear, nor has the eye seen any God besides you, who words for the one who waits for Him (Isaiah 64:4)

What God is sharing with us is that He, the Almighty, sovereign, omniscient, omnipresent, and omnipotent, will work for you if you truly and completely wait for Him. God invites you and me to be near Him and to stop trying to figure out how to live by our own strengths. He invites is to drop all our concerns, thoughts, and questions, and solely rest and wait for Him.

Can you do it?

Now faith is confidence in what we hope for and assurance about what we do not see.
—Hebrews 11:1

My sheep listen to my voice; I know them, and they follow me. I give them eternal life, and they shall never perish; no one will snatch them out of my hand.
—John 10:27–28

MY DAILY

Walk with God

And this is the testimony: God has given us eternal life, and this life is in his Son.
—1 John 5:11

(S) (M) (T) (W) (T) (F) (S)   **DATE:** _____

Reasons to Be Thankful

◯

◯

◯

◯

◯

◯

◯

Notes

- -

- -

- -

- -

- -

- -

- -

Self-Care Routine

❑ Get into nature; do something outside.

❑ Move your body for twenty minutes.

❑ Light some scented candles.

Every storm eventually runs out of rain; brighter days will come.

GOD

Heal my pain

I consider that our present sufferings are not worth comparing
with the glory that will be revealed in us.
—Romans 8:18

GOD
Heal my pain

So we fix our eyes not on what is seen, but on what is unseen, since
what is seen is temporary, but what is unseen is eternal.
—2 Corinthians 4:18

GOD

Heal my pain

But I trust in you, Lord
I say, "You are my God."
—Psalm 31:14

MY DAILY
Walk with God

For our light and momentary troubles are achieving for us an eternal glory that far outweighs them all.
—2 Corinthians 4:17

(S) (M) (T) (W) (T) (F) (S)   **DATE:** _____

New Things to Try

○

○

○

○

○

○

○

Self-Care Routine

❑ Buy some fresh flowers for your home.

❑ Take a shower.

Notes

- - - - - - - - - - - - - - - - - - - -

- - - - - - - - - - - - - - - - - - - -

- - - - - - - - - - - - - - - - - - - -

- - - - - - - - - - - - - - - - - - - -

- - - - - - - - - - - - - - - - - - - -

- - - - - - - - - - - - - - - - - - - -

- - - - - - - - - - - - - - - - - - - -

Suffering may be a chapter, but it's not the entire story of your life.

GOD
Heal my pain

Come to me, all you who are weary and burdened, and I will give you rest. Take my yoke upon you and learn from me, for I am gentle and humble in heart, and you will find rest for your souls. For my yoke is easy and my burden is light.
—Matthew 11:28–30

GOD
Heal my pain

If we died with him, we will also live with him;
—2 Timothy 2:11

MY DAILY
Walk with God

I have told you these things, so that in me you may have peace. In this world you will have trouble. But take heart! I have overcome the world.
—John 16:33

(S) (M) (T) (W) (T) (F) (S)   **DATE:** _____

Plans That Will Need Adjustments

○
○
○
○
○
○
○

Self-Care Routine

❑ Wash your bedding and towels.

❑ Take time to clean your house.

Notes

- - - - - - - - - - - - - - - - - - - -

- - - - - - - - - - - - - - - - - - - -

- - - - - - - - - - - - - - - - - - - -

- - - - - - - - - - - - - - - - - - - -

- - - - - - - - - - - - - - - - - - - -

- - - - - - - - - - - - - - - - - - - -

- - - - - - - - - - - - - - - - - - - -

In the face of death, may memories become a source of comfort.

GOD
Heal my pain

Happiness is not an emotion. It is not linked to material goods, trips, or moments. It also doesn't depend on someone to exist. People change, go far away, or pass away. How sad it would be if my happiness were fragilely connected to what is so ephemeral.

My happiness is in the eternal Rock, in the bread of life, in the owner of today and tomorrow, in the only one in whom there is no change or shadow of variation. I may not be smiling—yet—but my heart has rejoiced in the Lord.

Happiness is not an emotion. It is proof of my faith.

Where, O death, is your victory? Where, O death, is your sting? The sting of death is sin, and the power of sin is the law. But thanks be to God! He gives us the victory through our Lord Jesus Christ.
1 Corinthians 15:55–57

GOD
Heal my pain

Since ancient times no one has heard,
no ear has perceived, no eye has seen any God besides you,
who acts on behalf of those who wait for him.
—Isaiah 64:4

MY DAILY

Walk with God

My flesh and my heart may fail, but God is the strength of my heart and my portion forever.
—Psalm 73:26

(S) (M) (T) (W) (T) (F) (S)   **DATE:** _____

What feels good about your self-care routine?

○

○

○

○

○

○

Self-Care Routine

☐ Create a prayer corner.

☐ Go to the local library.

Notes

Death is not the end but a transition into eternity.

GOD
Heal my pain

But you, Lord, are a shield around me,
my glory, the One who lifts my head high.
—Psalm 3:3

GOD
Heal my pain

Do not be anxious about anything, but in every situation, by prayer and petition, with thanksgiving, present your requests to God. And the peace of God, which transcends all understanding, will guard your hearts and your minds in Christ Jesus.
—Philippians 4:6–7

GOD
Heal my pain

I can do all this through him who gives me strength.
—Philippians 4:13

GOD
Heal my pain

Now may the Lord of peace himself give you peace at all times
and in every way. The Lord be with all of you.
—2 Thessalonians 3:16

MY DAILY

Walk with God

Be strong and courageous. Do not be afraid or terrified because of them, for the Lord your God goes with you; he will never leave you nor forsake you.
—Deuteronomy 31:6

(S) (M) (T) (W) (T) (F) (S)

DATE: _____

Places That Make You Feel Safe

○

○

○

○

○

○

○

Self-Care Routine

❑ Write poetry.

❑ Have a movie night.

Share one memory about this place.

Cherish the moments shared for they become a timeless treasure.

GOD
Heal my pain

Be joyful in hope, patient in affliction, faithful in prayer.
—Romans 12:12

GOD
Heal my pain

When anxiety was great within me,
your consolation brought me joy.
—Psalm 94:19

MY DAILY
Walk with God

He heals the brokenhearted
and binds up their wounds.
—Psalm 147:3

(S) (M) (T) (W) (T) (F) (S)   **DATE:** _____

What is meaningful to you?

○
○
○
○
○
○
○

Self-Care Routine

☐ Stay in silence.

☐ Take a nap.

Notes

- - - - - - - - - - - - - - - - - - - -

- - - - - - - - - - - - - - - - - - - -

- - - - - - - - - - - - - - - - - - - -

- - - - - - - - - - - - - - - - - - - -

Bible Verses to Meditate on Today:

In the midst of sadness, may you find moments of quiet reflection and healing.

GOD

Heal my pain

A cheerful heart is good medicine, but a crushed spirit dries up the bones.
—Proverbs 17:22

MY DAILY
Walk with God

Even though I walk through the darkest valley, I will fear no evil, for you are with me; your rod and your staff, they comfort me.
—Psalm 23:4

(S) (M) (T) (W) (T) (F) (S)   **DATE:** _____

Insights You Gained from Your Pain:

- ○
- ○
- ○
- ○
- ○
- ○
- ○

What is God ministering to you?

Self-Care Routine

- ☐ Wash your face with cold water.
- ☐ Brew your morning coffee slowly.

Sadness is a visitor, not a permanent resident. It will pass.

MY DAILY
Walk with God

Surely your goodness and love will follow me all the days of my life, and I will dwell in the house of the Lord forever.
—Psalm 23:6

(S) (M) (T) (W) (T) (F) (S)   **DATE:** _____

Something to Be Thankful For:

○

○

○

○

○

○

○

Notes

- -

- -

- -

- -

- -

Call a friend!

Self-Care Routine

❑ Have a warm cup of coffee or tea.

❑ Get a body massage.

Let the tears flow, they carry the weight of healing and relief.

MY DAILY

Walk with God

The Lord is my shepherd,
I lack nothing.
——Psalm 23:1

(S) (M) (T) (W) (T) (F) (S)   **DATE:** _____

Friends I Can Call:

○

○

○

○

○

○

○

Self-Care Routine

❑ Clean your house.

❑ Do something physically
exerting: break down
cardboard boxes for recycling,
sprint to the end of the block.

Notes

- - - - - - - - - - - - - - - - - - -

- - - - - - - - - - - - - - - - - - -

- - - - - - - - - - - - - - - - - - -

- - - - - - - - - - - - - - - - - - -

- - - - - - - - - - - - - - - - - - -

Write a positive affirmation.

**Your feelings are valid, and
it's okay to give yourself the
time to navigate sadness.**

GOD
Heal my pain

You make known to me the path of life;
you will fill me with joy in your presence,
with eternal pleasures at your right hand.
—Psalm 16:11

MY DAILY
Walk with God

Come to me, all you who are weary and
burdened, and I will give you rest.
—Matthew 11:28

(S) (M) (T) (W) (T) (F) (S) **DATE:** _____

Bible Verses to Meditate On:

○
○
○
○
○
○
○

Self-Care Routine

❑ Get a lotion with your favorite
   scent.

❑ Take your meds.

❑ Take time to pray.

Notes

- - - - - - - - - - - - - - - - - - - -
- - - - - - - - - - - - - - - - - - - -
- - - - - - - - - - - - - - - - - - - -
- - - - - - - - - - - - - - - - - - - -
- - - - - - - - - - - - - - - - - - - -
- - - - - - - - - - - - - - - - - - - -
- - - - - - - - - - - - - - - - - - - -

**In Jesus, find the
anchor for your soul
during life's storms.**

GOD

Heal my pain

I wait for the Lord, my whole being waits,
and in his word I put my hope.
—Psalm 130:5

MY DAILY

Walk with God

But because of his great love for us, God, who is rich in mercy, made us alive with Christ even when we were dead in transgressions—it is by grace you have been saved.
—Ephesians 2:4–5

Ⓢ Ⓜ Ⓣ Ⓦ Ⓣ Ⓕ Ⓢ

DATE: _____

Prayer Request:

○

○

○

○

○

○

○

Notes

Who can pray for you?

Self-Care Routine

❑ Hug someone you love.

❑ Find a quiet place to pray.

Lean on the promises of Jesus, for they are wellspring of eternal hope.

GOD

Heal my pain

Have I not commanded you? Be strong and courageous. Do not be afraid; do not be discouraged, for the Lord your God will be with you wherever you go.
—Joshua 1:9

GOD
Heal my pain

May the God of hope fill you with all joy and peace as you trust in him, so
that you may overflow with hope by the power of the Holy Spirit.
—Romans 15:13

GOD

Heal my pain

I wait for the Lord, my whole being waits,
and in his word I put my hope.
—Psalm 130:5

GOD

Heal my pain

A friend loves at all times,
and a brother is born for a time of adversity.
—Proverbs 17:17

MY DAILY

Walk with God

But when you pray, go into your room, close the door and pray to your Father, who is unseen. Then your Father, who sees what is done in secret, will reward you.
—Matthew 6:6

(S) (M) (T) (W) (T) (F) (S)   **DATE:** _____

Movies that you want to watch:

○

○

○

○

○

○

○

Notes

- -

- -

- -

- -

- -

- -

- -

- -

Self-Care Routine

❑ How was the movie?

❑ Turn off your phone for one day.

❑ Enroll in therapy.

Jesus, the source of unwavering hope that sustains through every trial.

GOD

Heal my pain

God is not human, that he should lie, not a human being, that he should change his mind.
Does he speak and then not act? Does he promise and not fulfill?
—Number 23:19

GOD
Heal my pain

God, I don't have another option besides hiding myself under Your wings and surrendering to Your will. I don't have anywhere else to go. Remind me of your promises:

- He cares for me (1 Peter 5:7).
- He hears my distress and my cry (Psalm 120:1).
- He works for the One who waits for Him (Isaiah 64:4).
- He is not a man that He should lie, nor a son of man that He should repent (Numbers 23:19).

Keep going with God`s promises.

- -

- -

- -

- -

- -

What other promises do you need to be reminded of?

Cast all your anxiety on him because he cares for you.
—1 Peter 5:7

GOD
Heal my pain

But let all who take refuge in you be glad; let them ever sing for joy.
Spread your protection over them, that those who love your name may rejoice in you.
—Psalm 5:11

MY DAILY

Walk with God

But seek first his kingdom and his righteousness, and all these things will be given to you as well.
——Matthew 6:33

(S) (M) (T) (W) (T) (F) (S)   **DATE:** _____

Things you want to do:

○

○

○

○

○

○

○

Notes

- - - - - - - - - - - - -

- - - - - - - - - - - - -

- - - - - - - - - - - - -

- - - - - - - - - - - - -

- - - - - - - - - - - - -

Things you should do:

- Water a plant.
- Talk to a friend.

Self-Care Routine

❑ Snuggle your pets.

❑ Set a reminder to give yourself a positive affirmation sometime in the future.

Through Jesus, find a refuge of hope that stands firm in the face of adversity.

GOD

Heal my pain

There is a purpose in your suffering. You may not understand or agree with this right now. I don't have all the answers for my suffering, but every day God takes me near Him. In this season, I`m discovering that each day has enough trouble of its own.

For we live by faith, not by sight.
—2 Corinthians 5:7

MY DAILY

Walk with God

But you, Lord, are a shield around me,
my glory, the One who lifts my head high.
—Psalm 3:3

(S) (M) (T) (W) (T) (F) (S) **DATE:** _____

Reasons to move on with your life:

○
○
○
○
○
○
○

Self-Care Routine

❑ Visit a different place.

❑ Handwrite a note to your present self.

Notes

- - - - - - - - - - - - - - - - - - -
- - - - - - - - - - - - - - - - - - -
- - - - - - - - - - - - - - - - - - -
- - - - - - - - - - - - - - - - - - -
- - - - - - - - - - - - - - - - - - -
- - - - - - - - - - - - - - - - - - -
- - - - - - - - - - - - - - - - - - -

God loves us, and he holds us in our pain.
—Vaneetha Risner

GOD
Heal my pain

IT SHALL PASS

The Lord is my strength and my defense;
he has become my salvation.
—Psalm 118:14

GOD
Heal my pain

My flesh and my heart may fail, but God is the strength
of my heart and my portion forever.
—Psalm 73:26

MY DAILY

Walk with God

Surely God is my salvation; I will trust and not be afraid. The Lord, the Lord himself, is my strength and my defense; he has become my salvation.
—Isaiah 12:2

S M T W T F S

DATE: _____

Bible Verses to Meditate On:

○

○

○

○

○

○

○

Notes

- - - - - - - - - - - - - - - - - - - -

- - - - - - - - - - - - - - - - - - - -

- - - - - - - - - - - - - - - - - - - -

- - - - - - - - - - - - - - - - - - - -

- - - - - - - - - - - - - - - - - - - -

- - - - - - - - - - - - - - - - - - - -

- - - - - - - - - - - - - - - - - - - -

- - - - - - - - - - - - - - - - - - - -

Self-Care Routine

❑ Text a trusted friend how you're feeling.

❑ Think of a reason to be thankful.

**No matter what your situation may be, God is always with you. You are never completely alone when you know Christ.
—Billy Graham**

GOD
Heal my pain

Take delight in the Lord,
and he will give you the desires of your heart.
—Psalm 37:4

LORD MEET ME IN MY
Secret Place

God does not waste your pain.
What have you been learning in this season?

LORD MEET ME IN MY
Secret Place

Suddenly, God removed everything I wanted and planned for and started giving me what I needed most: His presence. Suddenly, He placed me in a position where there was no other option but to trust Him and believe He has better plans for me.

I still don't think it is fair, but I know my perspective is limited; I can only see so far. I see today, and I remember the past, but He sees tomorrow and prepares my future.

Cast all your anxiety on him because he cares for you.
—1 Peter 5:7

LORD MEET ME IN MY
Secret Place

There will be no intellectual satisfaction on this side of heaven to that age-old question, "Why?" But although I have not found intellectual satisfaction, I have found peace. And the answer I say to you is not an explanation but a person: Jesus Christ, my Lord and my God.
—Elizabeth Elliot

LORD MEET ME IN MY
Secret Place

God is not human, that he should lie, not a human
being, that he should change his mind.
Does he speak and then not act? Does he promise and not fulfill?
—Numbers 23:19

LORD MEET ME IN MY
Secret Place

Sometimes it is hard to accept God`s plans and permissions
for our lives. As David once did, you can also take time to cry
and ask some questions of God. Share your pain here.

Consider it pure joy, my brothers and sisters, whenever you face trials of many
kinds, because you know that the testing of your faith produces perseverance.
—James 1:2–3

LORD MEET ME IN MY
Secret Place

So we fix our eyes not on what is seen, but what is unseen.
For what is seen is temporary, but what is unseen is eternal.
—2 Corinthians 4:8

NOW IT'S TIME TO
Move on

When I say it's time to move on, I don't mean you should stop feeling your feelings or wipe your tears and start living your life as if everything was good with you. Moving on means trusting that God's plans are better than yours, laying down your pain at the cross, and allowing God to work in your life in this season.

In 2 Samuel 12:15–20, we find the following:

After Nathan had gone home, the LORD struck the child that Uriah's wife had borne to David, and he became ill. David pleaded with God for the child. He fasted and spent the nights lying in sackcloth[a] on the ground. The elders of his household stood beside him to get him up from the ground, but he refused, and he would not eat any food with them. On the seventh day the child died. David's attendants were afraid to tell him that the child was dead, for they thought, "While the child was still living, he wouldn't listen to us when we spoke to him. How can we now tell him the child is dead? He may do something desperate. David noticed that his attendants were whispering among themselves, and he realized the child was dead. "Is the child dead?" he asked.

"Yes," they replied, "he is dead."

Then David got up from the ground. After he had washed, put on lotions, and changed his clothes, he went into the house of the Lord and worshipped. Then he went to his own house, and at his request, they served him food, and he ate.

Here are some lessons I can learn from David's life:

1. You need to know when it's finished. Feel your feelings and allow yourself to cry. But start getting ready to move on. If you are not the one in the coffin, I can guarantee that God still has plans for you.

2. If God wanted to keep (insert name) alive, He would have! The fact that God did not do what you wanted Him to do doesn't mean He abandoned you!

3. Your faith needs to guide you when your answers end.

It is time to wash your face, change your clothes, make new plans, and let God be the Lord of your life.

NOW IT'S TIME TO
Move on

Write down your statement for a new life in Christ!

It Shall Pass!

Printed in the United States
by Baker & Taylor Publisher Services